Analogies
Grades 2–3

M000105751

Table of Contents

Introduction

Analogies build critical thinking and reasoning skills that are important in everyday learning as well as for standardized testing. Students can begin to learn the relationships shown in analogies by working with shape analogies, which show patterns, and then with picture analogies that compare familiar items. The thinking skills required to complete analogies are creative and higher level, encouraging students to think "out of the box." This kind of reasoning will strengthen students' thinking abilities across the curriculum and serve them throughout their lives in all kinds of activities.

ORGANIZATION AND USE

This book is divided into four units: Completing Analogies with Shapes, Completing Analogies with Pictures, Completing Word Analogies—Multiple Choice, and Completing Word Analogies—Supplying Words. The exercises progress from simplest to most difficult, and may be most effective when used in order; however, teachers may use any lesson at any time. Each two-page lesson has a sample exercise and an explanation of how the analogy should be read and completed. Some of the lessons in Unit Four are designed as one-page lessons so that students can complete smaller portions of these more difficult analogies.

At the end of each lesson is a short "Analogy-Wiz" exercise indicated by the "Wizard" icon. These exercises help stretch students' thinking and prepare them for the types of analogies that are to come in the book. There is also a one-page "Fun with Analogies" lesson at the end of units one through three.

Three assessments at the beginning of the book can be used as pre-tests or post-tests, or at any time a teacher wishes to gauge students' understanding of the lessons. The tests cover Completing Shape and Picture Analogies, Completing Word Analogies—Multiple Choice, and Supplying Words to Complete Analogies.

On page 3 is an Introduction to Analogies, which teachers should go over with their students before beginning. The Introduction describes what an analogy is, how it looks, and how it should be read. For the second and third grades, this book has introduced analogies using words, such as "is to" and "as." Later in the book, the symbols ":"and "::" are introduced. Teachers may wish to delay discussion of the symbols until students have had a chance to familiarize themselves with the analogies that use words.

The answer key gives answers as well as relationships to help teachers explain how to think through each analogy.

ADDITIONAL NOTES

Some Analogy-Wiz activities suggest partnering with a classmate or sharing with the class. Additional paper may be required in some cases.

Activities may be completed individually in class or as homework, in small groups or centers, or as a class. It is suggested that the teacher go over the examples and their solutions before having students work independently.

Analogies can be challenging, and they can also be fun. They are, in a sense, puzzles and brain teasers, and students' attitudes toward analogies can be positively influenced by treating the exercises this way. Encourage students to be creative, and be sure to keep an open mind. At times, there will be more than one right answer. If a student has a new answer, ask for an explanation. Through the explanation, the student will more clearly see the error of his or her thinking, or the teacher will see an interesting new solution!

Name _____ Date _____

Introduction to Analogies

An analogy is a way of comparing things.
An analogy has two parts, joined by the word **AS**.

This is a picture analogy:

 is to **AS** is to

This analogy compares how the fish and bowl are like the bird and cage. A goldfish lives in a fish bowl. A parakeet lives in a bird cage.

This is a word analogy:

green is to grass **AS** blue is to sky

This analogy compares how green and grass are like blue and the sky. Green is the color of grass. Blue is the color of the sky.

Read this word analogy. Which word from the box completes the analogy?

dog is to puppy **AS** cat is to _____

baby	kitten	meow

 Think: A puppy is a baby dog. Which word in the word box is the same to a cat as the puppy is to a dog?

Answer: A kitten is a baby cat, so **kitten** is the correct choice to complete the analogy.

An analogy can have symbols instead of words. It can look like this:

dog : bark :: cat : meow   : means **is to**   :: means **AS**

Now try these:

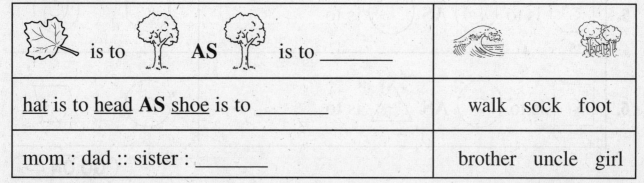

www.svschoolsupply.com
© Steck-Vaughn Company

Shape and Picture Analogies

Directions Look at the shapes. Choose the shape that will complete the analogy. Circle it.

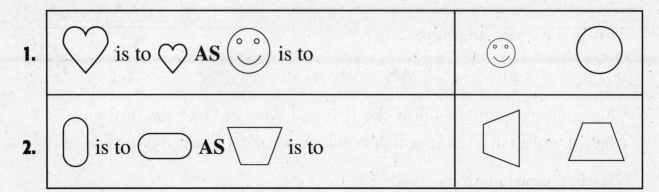

1. ♡ is to ♡ **AS** ☺ is to   ☺   ◯

2. ▯ is to ⬭ **AS** ⏢ is to   ◁   ⏢

Directions Color all of the shapes. Then, choose the colored shape that will complete the analogy. Circle it.

3. ◇ is to ◇ **AS** ☾ is to

   green   yellow   green   yellow   white

4. ☆ is to ☆ **AS** ◯ is to

   red   orange   red   orange   orange

Directions Look at the shapes. Then, choose the shape that will complete the analogy. Circle it.

5. ⬡ is to 🌀 **AS** ◯ is to   ⬡   🌀

6. ▫ is to ◉ **AS** △ is to   ◉   ▱

Shape and Picture Analogies

(Directions) **Choose a pair of shapes to complete the analogy. Circle the letter under the pair you choose.**

7.
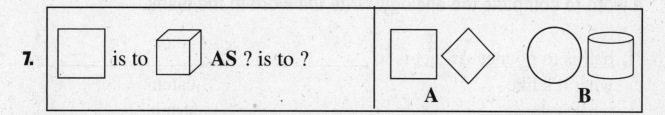

(Directions) **Look at the first two pictures. Decide how they compare. Choose a picture that compares to the third picture in the same way. Circle your choice.**

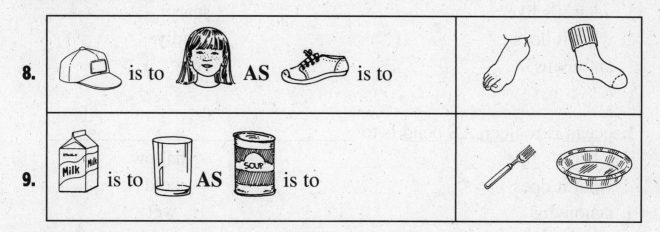

8.

9.

(Directions) **Look at the first two pictures. Decide how they compare. Choose a picture from the box that compares to the third picture in the same way. Write the letter of your choice in the blank.**

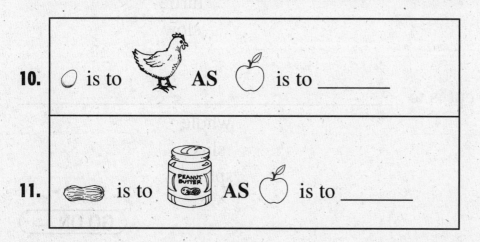

10. is to AS is to _____

11. is to AS is to _____

Word Analogies

(Directions) Read each analogy. Decide how the first pair of words is related. Circle the word or words that tell what kind of analogy it is. Choose a word to complete the analogy. Write the word in the blank.

1. <u>ball</u> is to <u>bounce</u> **AS** <u>net</u> is to _____

what it's like	catch
what it does	string
synonyms	light

2. <u>baby</u> is to <u>small</u> **AS** <u>giant</u> is to _____

what it's like	scary
what it does	friendly
antonyms	big

3. <u>ocean</u> is to <u>deep</u> **AS** <u>pond</u> is to _____

what it's like	shallow
what it does	cold
synonyms	wet

4. <u>rough</u> is to <u>smooth</u> **AS** <u>fast</u> is to _____

what it's like	quick
what it does	turtle
antonyms	slow

5. <u>mix</u> is to <u>stir</u> **AS** <u>cut</u> is to _____

what it's like	whole
what it does	slice
synonyms	spread

GO ON ⇨

Word Analogies

Directions Read each analogy. Choose a second analogy pair that compares in the same way as the first pair. Circle the pair you choose.

6. bulb : light ::   sun : sky   cord : power

7. egg : carton ::   soup : can   corn : garden   Eggs

8. bed : sleep ::   table : eat   chair : table

9. rose : red ::   cloud : white   cloud : high

10. police : safety ::   doctor : white   postal worker : mail

Directions Read each analogy. Choose a second analogy pair that compares in the same way as the first pair. Draw a line to connect the matching pairs.

11. plants : garden ::   air : plane

12. uncle : aunt ::   desert : sand

13. rail : train ::   front : back

14. mountain top : snow ::   trees : woods

15. cat : meow ::   brother : sister

16. high : low ::   dog : bark

Name _____ Date _____

In Your Own Words

Directions Read each analogy. Think about how the first word pair is related. Think of a word to go with the third word that relates to it in the same way. Write the word.

1. sink : wash :: bed : _____

2. ear : head :: toe : _____

3. office : work :: playground : _____

4. people : doctor :: pets : _____

5. eyes : see :: ears : _____

6. pig : wig :: top : _____

Directions Read each analogy. Think about how the second word pair is related. Think of a word to go with the first word that relates to it in the same way. Write the word.

7. lose : _____ :: give : take

8. pants : _____ :: shirt : arms

9. books : _____ :: movies : watch

10. car : _____ :: train : rails

11. flame : _____ :: ice : freeze

12. dark : _____ :: day : night

GO ON ⇒

www.svschoolsupply.com
© Steck-Vaughn Company

8

Assessment: Supplying Words to Complete Analogies
Analogies 2-3, SV 6906-X

In Your Own Words

Directions Read each analogy. Think about how the first word pair is related. Think of a word to go with the last word that relates to it in the same way. Write the word.

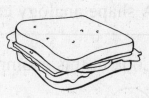

13. money : bank :: _____ : post office

14. cake : bakery :: _____ : book store

15. glass : juice :: _____ : sandwich

16. pickle : sour :: _____ : sweet

17. wing : swing :: _____ : ride

18. foggy : clear :: _____ : sunny

Directions Read each analogy. Think about how the second word pair is related. Think of a word to go with the second word that relates to it in the same way. Write the word.

19. _____ : brick :: smooth : window

20. _____ : shampoo :: body : soap

21. _____ : quiet :: ceiling : floor

22. _____ : house :: bench : park

23. _____ : ice :: sled : snow

24. _____ : tug :: push : shove

Looking at Sizes

A shape analogy can be based on sizes.

Look at this example:

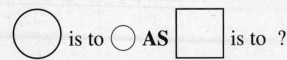

○ is to ○ **AS** ☐ is to ?

 THINK: What would complete this analogy? Compare the first two shapes. How are they alike? How are the different? What shape would compare in the same way?

Answer: The first two shapes are both circles, but the second one is smaller than the first one. The next shape is a large square. A smaller square would complete this analogy.

○ is to ○ **AS** ☐ is to ☐

(**Directions**) **Look at the shapes. Choose the shape that will complete the analogy. Circle it.**

1.	♡ is to ♡ **AS** △ is to	♡ △
2.	☺ is to ☺ **AS** ⬡ is to	⬡ ⊘
3.	⚡ is to ⚡ **AS** ☺ is to	♡ ☺

(**GO ON** ⇒)

Looking at Sizes

(Directions) Look at the shapes. Choose the shape that will complete the analogy. Circle it.

4. ⬯ is to ⬯ **AS** ✚ is to	⬡ ✚
5. ◺ is to ◺ **AS** ◯ is to	◯ ◹
6. ⌒ is to ⌒ **AS** ▯ is to	▭ ▬
7. ⬠ is to ⬠ **AS** ◺ is to	◹ ◿

Analogy-Wiz

Draw your own shape analogy. Share it with a classmate.

_____ is to _____ **AS** _____ is to _____

Looking at Colors

A shape analogy can be based on colors.

Look at this example:

○ is to ○ **AS** □ is to ?
red   blue   red

 THINK: What would complete this analogy? Another red circle? A blue circle? Or a different shape and color?

Answer: Another blue square would complete this analogy.

○ is to ○ **AS** □ is to □
red   blue   red   blue

(Directions) **Color all of the shapes. Then, choose the colored shape that will complete the analogy. Circle it.**

1. ☾ is to ☾ **AS** △ is to yellow green yellow	△ △ red green
2. ☆ is to ☆ **AS** ○ is to white blue white	○ ☆ blue blue

(GO ON ⇨)

Name _____   Date _____

Looking at Colors

Directions Color all of the shapes. Then, choose the colored shape that will complete the analogy. Circle it.

3. ⬆ is to ⬆ **AS** ◇ is to orange red orange	◇ ◯ red red
4. ♡ is to ♡ **AS** ☆ is to red yellow red	♡ ☆ yellow yellow
5. ✚ is to ✚ **AS** ☾ is to red blue red	☾ ☾ red blue
6. ◯ is to ◯ **AS** ➡ is to blue black blue	➡ ➡ blue black

Analogy-Wiz

Draw your own colored shape analogy. Share it with a classmate.

_____ is to _____   **AS**   _____ is to _____

13

Looking at Designs

A shape analogy can be based on designs.

Look at this example:

 is to **AS** is to ?

 THINK: What would complete this analogy? Another plain circle? A square? Or a different shape with a design?

Answer: A plain square would complete this analogy.

 is to **AS** is to

(Directions) Look at the shapes. Then, choose the shape that will complete the analogy. Circle it.

1.	
2. 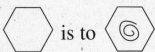	

(GO ON ⇒)

Looking at Designs

Directions Look at the shapes. Then, choose the shape that will complete the analogy. Circle it.

3.	⬡(with X) is to ⬡(with X lines) **AS** ⋈ is to	⋈ ⬡(with X)
4.	◇(with line) is to ◇(with S) **AS** ▱(with line) is to	◇(with line) ▱(with S)
5.	⊞ is to ⊠ **AS** ⊟ is to	⊟ ⊠(rectangle)
6.	♡(with circle) is to ∞(with circle) **AS** ♡ is to	♡(with circle) ∞

Analogy-Wiz

Draw your own shape analogy with a design. Leave the last line blank for a classmate to fill in.

_____ is to _____ **AS** _____ is to _____

Doubling Up

To complete these analogies, you will need to choose a pair of shapes. The two shapes you choose will complete an analogy.

Look at this example:

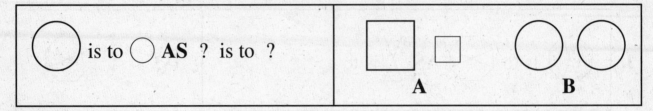

 **THINK:** How are the first two shapes the same? How are they different? Which pair of shapes in the box is alike and different in the same way?

Answer: The shapes are both circles. One is big, and the other is small. **A** shows two squares. One is big, and the other is small. **B** shows two circles. They are both the same size. **A** compares more closely with the first two shapes, so **A** completes this analogy.

(Directions) **Choose a pair of shapes to complete the analogy. Circle the letter under the pair you choose.**

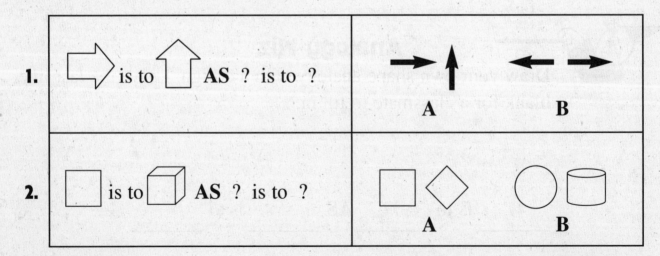

Unit One: Shape Combinations
Analogies 2-3, SV 6906-X

Doubling Up

Directions Choose a pair of shapes to complete the analogy. Circle the letter under the pair you choose.

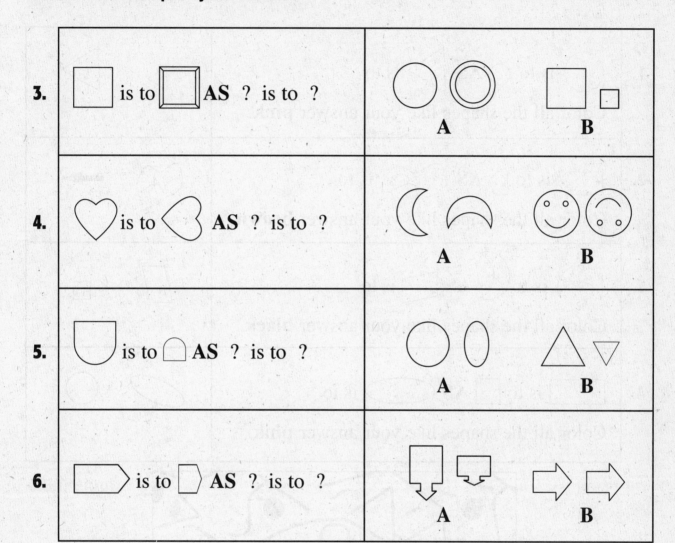

Analogy-Wiz

Draw your own shape analogy with two pair choices. Trade with a classmate to complete.

_____ is to _____ **AS** ? is to ?

_____   A   B

Pretty in Pink

(Directions) Complete each shape analogy. Circle your answer. Then, color the shapes in the puzzle that match the answer shapes to find Pearl!

1. ◯ is to ◯ **AS** ▷ is to ____

Color all the shapes like your answer **pink**.

2. ⬠ is to ⬠ **AS** ∿ is to ____

Color all the shapes like your answer **brown**.

3. ☾ is to ☽ **AS** ▱ is to ____

Color all the shapes like your answer **black**.

4. ▭ is to ▢ **AS** ⬭ is to ____

Color all the shapes like your answer **pink**.

Picture This

A picture analogy uses pictures to take the place of words.

Look at this example:

 is to  **AS** is to |

 THINK: Compare the first two pictures. How are they alike? How are they different? Which picture from the box compares to a kitten in the same way?

Answer: A **chick** is a baby **chicken**. A **kitten** is a baby **cat**. **Cat** completes this analogy.

(**Directions**) Look at the first two pictures. Decide how they compare. Choose a picture that compares to the third picture in the same way. Circle your choice.

1. is to **AS** is to |

2. 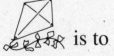 is to **AS** is to |

GO ON ⇨

Picture This

Directions Look at the first two pictures. Decide how they compare. Choose a picture that compares to the third picture in the same way. Circle your choice.

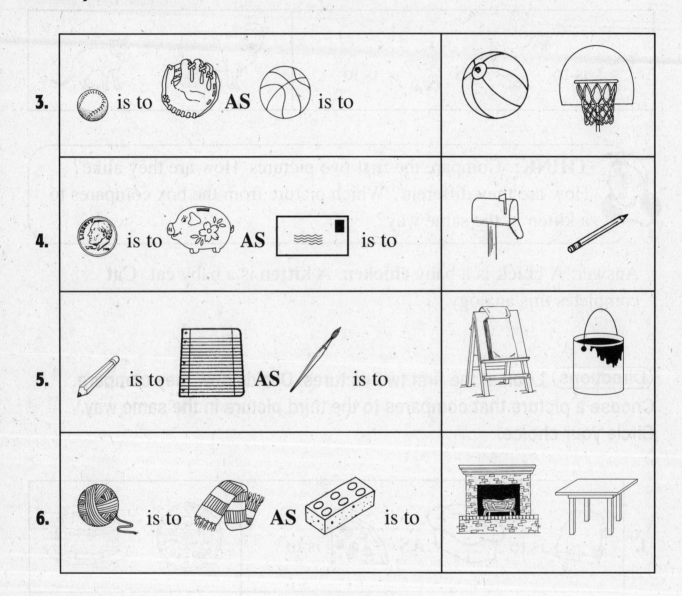

Analogy-Wiz
Draw your own picture analogy. Explain your drawing to a classmate or a family member.

Choosing from a Group

A picture analogy uses pictures to take the place of words.

Look at this example:

 is to **AS** is to _____

 THINK: Compare the first two pictures. How are they related? Which picture from the box compares to a couch in the same way?

Answer: A **bed** is found in a **bedroom**. A **couch** is found in a **living room**, so **living room** completes this analogy.

(**Directions**) Look at the first two pictures in each row. Decide how they compare. Choose a picture from the box that compares to the third picture in the same way. Write the letter of your choice in the blank.

1.

2.

GO ON ⇨

Choosing from a Group

Directions Look at the first two pictures in each row. Decide how they are related. Choose a picture from the box that compares to the third picture in the same way. Write the letter of your choice in the blank.

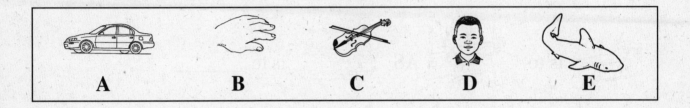

A   B   C   D   E

3.  is to _____

4.  are to _____

5. 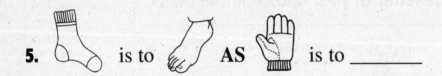 is to _____

6.  is to _____

Analogy-Wiz

Think of an analogy that compares your senses and what they do (like number 4 does). Share your analogy with your class.

Looking for Rhymes

A rhyme analogy compares words that have the same sound.

Look at this example:

 is to **AS**  is to

dog   frog   fox   snake   box

 THINK: The word **dog** has the same sound, or rhymes, with the word **frog**. Which word in the box rhymes with the word **fox**?

Answer: The word **box** rhymes with the word **fox**, so **box** completes this analogy.

(Directions) **Read each analogy. Choose a picture from the box whose name rhymes with the third picture name. Write the picture name in the blank.**

snake   clock   top   horn

1. is to **AS** ◻️ is to _____

boy   toy   block

2. is to ☐ **AS** is to _____

bear   square   corn

3. is to **AS** is to _____

carrot   parrot   cake

(GO ON ⇨)

Looking for Rhymes

Directions Read each analogy. Choose a picture from the box whose name rhymes with the third picture name. Write the picture name in the blank.

| squirrel | nose | cub | bee | baby | whale |

4.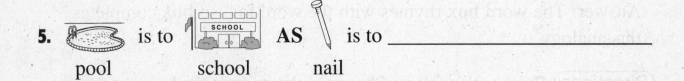

hat   is to   cat   **AS**   tree   is to _____

5.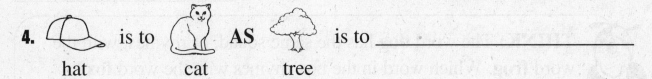

pool   is to   school   **AS**   nail   is to _____

6.

rope   is to   soap   **AS**   hose   is to _____

7.

cut   is to   nut   **AS**   girl   is to _____

8.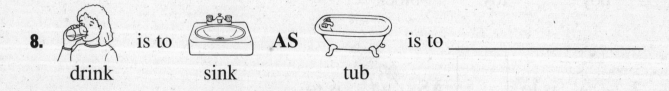

drink   is to   sink   **AS**   tub   is to _____

Analogy-Wiz

Draw a picture analogy that rhymes. Share your analogy with your class.

Looking for Opposites

Some analogies compare opposites.

Look at this example:

<u>light</u> is to <u>dark</u> **AS** <u>day</u> is to

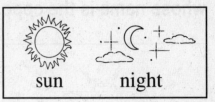

sun   night

THINK: Light is the opposite of dark. Which picture in the box shows something that is the opposite of day?

Answer: The sun shines during the day, but **sun** is not the opposite of day. **Night** is the opposite of **day**, so **night** completes this analogy.

(Directions) **Read each analogy. Choose a picture from the picture box whose name is the opposite of the third word. Write the word in the blank.**

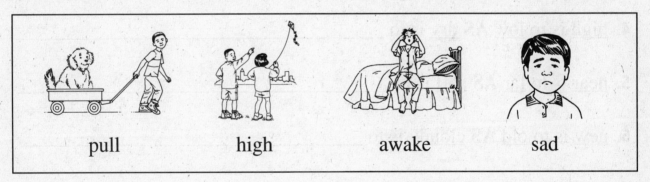

pull   high   awake   sad

1. <u>work</u> is to <u>play</u> **AS** <u>asleep</u> is to _____

2. <u>sink</u> is to <u>float</u> **AS** <u>happy</u> is to _____

3. <u>up</u> is to <u>down</u> **AS** <u>push</u> is to _____

(GO ON ⇒)

Looking for Opposites

(**Directions**) **Read each analogy. Choose a picture from the picture box whose name is the opposite of the third word. Write the word in the blank.**

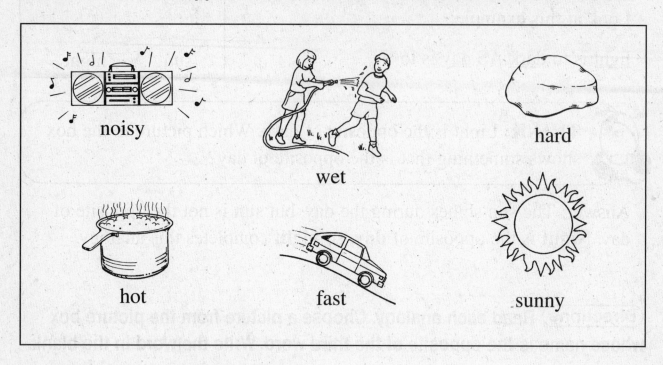

noisy

wet

hard

hot

fast

sunny

4. <u>high</u> is to <u>low</u> **AS** <u>dry</u> is to _____

5. <u>near</u> is to <u>far</u> **AS** <u>soft</u> is to _____

6. <u>new</u> is to <u>old</u> **AS** <u>cloudy</u> is to _____

7. <u>break</u> is to <u>fix</u> **AS** <u>quiet</u> is to _____

8. <u>give</u> is to <u>take</u> **AS** <u>cold</u> is to _____

Analogy-Wiz

Choose a classmate as a partner. Write an analogy that compares opposite ways of feeling or being. Act out your analogy for the rest of your class. Say **is to** and **AS**, but do not say the words you are comparing. See if your class can guess what the words are.

Name _____ Date _____

Every Picture Tells a Story!

(Directions) Complete these analogies by circling the correct picture. Then, look at all the pictures you circled. Imagine how the pictures could be connected. Write a short story about all of the pictures. Share your story with your class.

1. <u>woman</u> is to <u>man</u> **AS** <u>girl</u> is to ?

2. <u>ice cream</u> is to <u>boy</u> **AS** <u>bone</u> is to ?

3. <u>dirty</u> is to <u>mud puddle</u> **AS** <u>clean</u> is to ?

4. <u>feathers</u> are to <u>bird</u> **AS** <u>fur</u> is to ?

_____

_____

_____

_____

_____

_____

_____

_____

Deciding How Things Relate

An analogy can compare how things look or feel.
Or it can compare what things do.

Look at this example:

bat is to hit **AS** mitt is to _____   ball   catch

THINK: How do bat and hit relate to each other? Hit is what a bat does. What does a mitt do?

Answer: A mitt catches, so **catch** completes this analogy.

Now look at this example:

pillow is to soft **AS** rock is to _____   hard   round

THINK: How do pillow and soft relate to each other? A pillow feels soft. How does a rock feel?

Answer: A **rock** feels **hard**, so **hard** completes this analogy.

(Directions) **Read each analogy. Decide if the first pair is comparing how things look or feel, or what they do. Circle the words that tell what kind of analogy it is. Choose a word to complete the analogy. Write the word in the blank.**

1. glass is to smooth **AS** sandpaper is to _____
look/feel   wood   rough
what they do

2. oven is to bake **AS** saw is to _____
look/feel   cut   sharp
what they do

(GO ON ⇨)

Deciding How Things Relate

Directions Read each analogy. Decide if the first pair is comparing how things look or feel, or what they do. Circle the words that tell what kind of analogy it is. Choose a word to complete the analogy. Write the word in the blank.

3. <u>bird</u> is to <u>fly</u> **AS** <u>ant</u> is to _____
look/feel   small   crawl
what they do

4. <u>ear</u> is to <u>hear</u> **AS** <u>eye</u> is to _____
look/feel   see   face
what they do

5. <u>flame</u> is to <u>hot</u> **AS** <u>ice</u> is to _____
look/feel   cube   cold
what they do

6. <u>ocean</u> is to <u>blue</u> **AS** <u>sun</u> is to _____
look/feel   shine   yellow
what they do

7. <u>teeth</u> are to <u>chew</u> **AS** <u>tongue</u> is to _____
look/feel   taste   red
what they do

Analogy-Wiz

An analogy can use symbols instead of words.
: means **is to**, and :: means **AS**.

Directions Draw a line to match the first pair of each analogy to a second pair that compares in the same way.

broom : sweep ::   day : light

night : dark ::   sponge : wash

Different or the Same?

An analogy can compare words that are opposites, or it can compare words that mean the same thing. Words that mean the opposite are **antonyms**. Words that mean the same thing are **synonyms**.

Look at this example:

<u>sad</u> is to <u>unhappy</u> **AS** <u>glad</u> is to _____   mad   smile   happy

THINK: Sad means the same thing as **unhappy**. These words are synonyms. Which word means the same thing as **glad**?

Answer: You may smile when you are glad, but **smile** does not mean the same thing as glad. The word that means the same thing as glad is **happy**, so **happy** completes this analogy.

Look at this example:

<u>tall</u> is to <u>short</u> **AS** <u>thick</u> is to _____   thin   heavy   flat

THINK: Tall is the opposite of **short**. These words are antonyms. Which word is the opposite of **thick**?

Answer: The word that means the opposite of **thick** is **thin**, so **thin** completes this analogy.

(Directions) **Decide if the first two words in the analogy are antonyms or synonyms. Circle one. Then, choose a word from the word box to complete the analogy. Write it on the line.**

| lock | close | slow | quick |

1. <u>smooth</u> is to <u>rough</u> **AS** <u>fast</u> is to _____
   antonyms
   synonyms

(GO ON ⇨)

Name _____ Date _____

Different or the Same?

(Directions) Decide if the first two words are antonyms or synonyms. Circle one. Then, choose a word from the word box to complete the analogy. Write it on the line.

hop	fall	back	hear	go	ocean

2. <u>stay</u> is to <u>remain</u> **AS** <u>leave</u> is to _____
antonyms
synonyms

3. <u>talk</u> is to <u>speak</u> **AS** <u>listen</u> is to _____
antonyms
synonyms

4. <u>top</u> is to <u>bottom</u> **AS** <u>front</u> is to _____
antonyms
synonyms

5. <u>dry</u> is to <u>wet</u> **AS** <u>desert</u> is to _____
antonyms
synonyms

Analogy-Wiz

An analogy can use symbols instead of words.
: means **is to**, and :: means **AS**.

(Directions) Draw a line to match the first pair of each analogy to a second pair that compares in the same way.

blossom : flower ::   right : wrong

left : right ::   dirt : soil

What It Does or What It's Like?

Some analogies compare what things or people do. Others compare what things are like, or their characteristics.

Look at this example:

<u>pilot</u> is to <u>fly</u> **AS** <u>author</u> is to _____   book   write   plane

THINK: A pilot flies. This tells what a pilot does. Which word tells what an author does?

Answer: An author works with books, but what an author does is **write**. So **write** completes this analogy.

Look at this example:

<u>white</u> is to <u>milk</u> **AS** <u>yellow</u> is to _____   color   banana   bright

THINK: White describes what milk is like. White is a characteristic of milk. Which word is yellow a characteristic of?

Answer: Yellow is a color, but it is not a characteristic of color. Yellow may be bright, but it is not a characteristic of bright. **Yellow** is a characteristic of a **banana**, so **banana** completes this analogy.

(Directions) Decide if the first word pair compares what someone or something does or what something is like (its characteristic). Circle one. Then, choose a word from the word box to complete the analogy. Write it on the line.

close   measure   fix   ride

1. <u>key</u> is to <u>open</u> **AS** <u>cup</u> is to _____
   what it does
   what it's like

GO ON ⇒

Name _____ Date _____

What It Does or What It's Like?

(Directions) Decide if the first word pair compares what someone or something does or what something is like (its characteristic). Circle one. Then, choose a word from the word box to complete the analogy. Write it on the line.

| easel | round | frog | bounce | paint | mouse |

2. <u>box</u> is to <u>square</u> **AS** <u>ball</u> is to _____
what it does
what it's like

3. <u>huge</u> is to <u>elephant</u> **AS** <u>tiny</u> is to _____
what it does
what it's like

4. <u>moo</u> is to <u>cow</u> **AS** <u>croak</u> is to _____
what it does
what it's like

5. <u>doctor</u> is to <u>cure</u> **AS** <u>artist</u> is to _____
what someone does
what someone is like

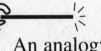 ## Analogy-Wiz

An analogy can use symbols instead of words.
: means **is to**, and :: means **AS**.

(Directions) Draw a line to match the first pair of each analogy to a second pair that compares in the same way.

hiker : walk ::   diver : swim

summer : hot ::   winter : cold

Parts of a Whole

Some analogies compare parts to a whole.
An analogy can use symbols instead of words.
: means **is to**, and :: means **AS**.

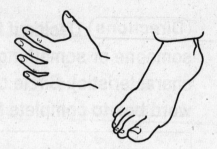

Look at this example:

finger : hand :: _____ : _____   walk : foot   toe: foot

THINK: Fingers are part of a hand. They are both parts of a body. Which word pair compares other body parts in the same way?

Answer: You walk on your foot, but walking is not part of a foot. A **toe** is part of a **foot**, so **toe : foot** completes this analogy.

(Directions) Choose a second analogy pair that compares in the same way as the first pair. Circle the pair you choose.

1. tree : forest ::   flower : garden   cloud : sky

2. fish : school ::   cow : calf   deer : herd

3. letter : alphabet ::   page : book   bench : park

4. mountain : range ::   arm : hand   dune : desert

Analogy-Wiz

Think of two analogy pairs that go together. Write the analogy using :, ::, and :. Write a sentence that explains why your analogy pairs go together.

_____

_____

Connecting Pairs of Analogies

(**Directions**) Read each analogy pair. Think about how the first pair compares. They may be antonyms or synonyms, they may describe, they may tell what something does, or they may be parts of a whole. Choose a second analogy pair that compares in the same way as the first pair. Draw a line to connect the pairs.

1. boy : girl ::

2. wood : house ::

3. saw : cut ::

4. bird : flock ::

5. teacher : class ::

6. star : sky ::

7. look : see ::

8. letter : paper ::

a. whale : pod

b. email : computer

c. leader : band

d. father : mother

e. shell : beach

f. dough : crust

g. shovel : dig

h. listen : hear

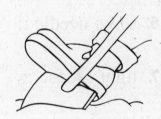

Analogy-Wiz

Think of two analogy pairs that go together. Write the analogy using :, ::, and :. Write a sentence that explains why your analogy pairs go together.

_____

_____

Connecting Pairs of Analogies

Directions Read each analogy pair. Think about how the first pair compares. They may be antonyms or synonyms, they may describe, they may tell what something does, or they may be parts of a whole. Choose a second analogy pair that compares in the same way as the first pair. Draw a line to connect the pairs.

1. bee : honey ::

2. person : family ::

3. astronaut : space ::

4. nurse : hospital ::

5. dry : sand ::

6. sew : needle ::

7. tight : loose ::

8. hard : difficult ::

a. sailor : sea

b. boring : interesting

c. measure : ruler

d. wet : water

e. cow : milk

f. easy : simple

g. lion : pride

h. teacher : school

Analogy-Wiz

Think of two analogy pairs that go together. Write the analogy using :, ::, and :. Write a sentence that explains why your analogy pairs go together.

_____

_____

Don't Bug Me!

Directions To complete this crossword, you will need to complete the analogies. Fill in the blank for each analogy, then write the words in the puzzle. All of the analogies are about creepy-crawlers!

| moth | ladybug | grasshopper | bee | spider | butterfly | ant |

ACROSS

1. <u>bow</u> is to <u>violin</u> **AS** <u>wings</u> are to _____

6. <u>tadpole</u> is to <u>frog</u> **AS** <u>caterpillar</u> is to _____

DOWN

2. <u>nest</u> is to <u>bird</u> **AS** <u>hill</u> is to _____

3. <u>magnet</u> is to <u>metal</u> **AS** <u>light</u> is to _____

4. <u>egg</u> is to <u>chicken</u> **AS** <u>egg sac</u> is to _____

5. <u>stripe</u> is to <u>hornet</u> **AS** <u>spots</u> are to _____

6. <u>silk</u> is to <u>silkworm</u> **AS** <u>honey</u> is to _____

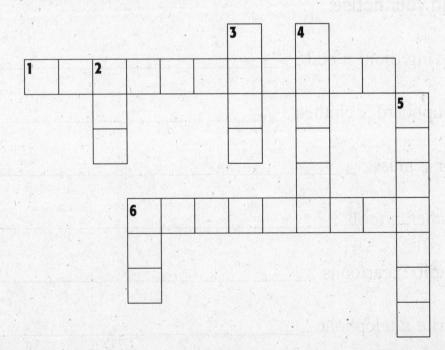

The Last Word

To complete these analogies, you will have to supply the last word from words that you know.

Look at this example:

bathtub : bathroom :: stove : _____

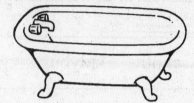

 **THINK:** How are a bathtub and bathroom related? A bathroom is the room where you would find a bathtub. In which room would you find a stove?

Answer: You would probably find a **stove** in the **kitchen**, so **kitchen** completes this analogy.

(**Directions**) Read each analogy. Think about how the first word pair is related. Think of a word to go with the third word that relates to it in the same way. All of the analogies on this page are about things you see in or around your house.

1. couch : living room :: bed : _____

2. dishes : cupboard :: clothes : _____

3. rug : floor :: grass : _____

4. food : kitchen :: tools : _____

5. music : radio :: cartoons : _____

6. email : write :: telephone : _____

Name _____ Date _____

The Last Word

Directions Read each analogy. Think about how the first word pair is related. Think of a word to go with the third word that relates to it in the same way. All of the analogies on this page are about different places on Earth.

1. moist : rain forest :: dry : _____

2. snow : arctic :: grass : _____

3. trees : forest :: sea shells : _____

4. frog : pond :: whale : _____

5. gopher : prairie :: raccoon : _____

6. seaweed : ocean :: cactus : _____

7. shark : ocean :: camel : _____

8. polar bear : cold :: desert rat : _____

Analogy-Wiz

Write two analogies about Earth. Leave out the last word for a classmate to complete.

The Second Word

To complete these analogies, you will have to supply the second word from words that you know.

Look at this example:

librarian : _____ :: florist : flowers

THINK: How are the second pair of words related? A florist works with flowers. What does a librarian work with?

Answer: A **librarian** works with **books**, so **books** completes this analogy.

(Directions) Read each analogy. Think about how the second word pair is related. Think of a word to go with the first word that relates to it in the same way. All of the analogies on this page are about different types of jobs.

1. money : _____ :: tools : carpenter

2. flour : _____ :: cloth : tailor

3. nails : _____ :: cement : bricklayer

4. artist : _____ :: musician : instrument

5. woodcutter : _____ :: writer : pen

6. classroom : _____ :: boat : captain

The Second Word

(**Directions**) Read each analogy. Think about how the second word pair is related. Think of a word to go with the first word that relates to it in the same way. All of the analogies on this page are about what things do.

1. scissors : _____ :: glue : connect

2. pencil : _____ :: eraser : erase

3. broom : _____ :: towel : dry

4. oven : _____ :: freezer : freeze

5. screwdriver : _____ :: hammer : hit

6. wind : _____ :: sun : shine

7. shovel : _____ :: cup : measure

8. knife : _____ :: spoon : stir

Analogy-Wiz

Write two analogies about what things or people do. Leave out the second word for a classmate to complete.

The Third Word

To complete these analogies, you will have to supply the third word from words that you know.

Look at this example:

crayon : color :: _____ : write

 THINK: How are the first pair of words related? You color with a crayon. What do you write with?

Answer: You **write** with a **pen** or a **pencil**, so either **pen** or **pencil** could complete this analogy.

(Directions) Read each analogy. Think about how the first word pair is related. Think of a word to go with the last word that relates to it in the same way. All of the analogies on this page are about what people do with or to things.

1. climb : mountain :: _____ : bike

2. chew : food :: _____ : water

3. drive : car :: _____ : train

4. mow : lawn :: _____ : leaves

5. watch : TV :: _____ : radio

6. plant : seeds :: _____ : weeds

The Third Word

(**Directions**) Read each analogy. Think about how the first word pair is related. Think of a word to go with the last word that relates to it in the same way. All of the analogies on this page are about what people do with or to things.

1. climb : tree :: _____ : lake

2. ski : snow :: _____ : ice

3. comb : hair :: _____ : teeth

4. write : letter :: _____ : newspaper

5. hose : spray :: _____ : pour

6. shop : store :: _____ : park

7. push : stroller :: _____ : wagon

8. flip : switch :: _____ : knob

Analogy-Wiz
Write two analogies about what people do with or to things.
Leave out the third word for a classmate to complete.

The First Word

To complete these analogies, you will have to supply the first word from words that you know.

Look at this example:

_____ : snow :: green : grass

 THINK: How are the second pair of words related? Green describes the color of grass. What word describes the color of snow?

Answer: **Snow** is **white**, so **white** completes this analogy.

(Directions) Read each analogy. Think about how the second word pair is related. Think of a word to go with the second word that relates to it in the same way. All of the analogies on this page describe, or tell about, things.

1. _____ : fire :: cold : ice

2. _____ : sky :: low : ground

3. _____ : bird :: wool : sheep

4. _____ : watch :: wall : clock

5. _____ : apple :: vegetable : pea

6. _____ : block :: round : baseball

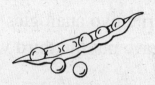

The First Word

(Directions) Read each analogy. Think about how the second word pair is related. Think of a word to go with the second word that relates to it in the same way. All of the analogies on this page describe, or tell about, things.

1. _____ : lemon :: green : lime

2. _____ : tree :: scales : fish

3. _____ : fish :: walk : horse

4. _____ : clock :: temperature : thermometer

5. _____ : car :: handlebars : bicycle

6. _____ : paper :: nails : wood

7. _____ : picture :: fence : yard

8. _____ : finger :: bracelet : wrist

Analogy-Wiz

Write two analogies that describe, or tell about, things. Leave out the first word for a classmate to complete.

Analogies
Grades 2-3

Answer Key

page 3
forest   foot   brother

pages 4–5
1. first picture; large to small
2. first picture; right-side-up to sideways
3. yellow moon
4. orange circle
5. second picture; plain shape to shape with design inside
6. second picture; first pair both have circle in center; second pair both have heart at bottom
7. B; 2-D figure to 3-D figure
8. foot; where it is worn
9. bowl; how it is served
10. C; where it comes from
11. A; what it makes

pages 6–7
1. what it does; catch
2. what it's like; big
3. what it's like; shallow
4. antonyms; slow
5. synonyms; slice
6. cord : power; what they do
7. soup : can; how they are packaged
8. table : eat; where we do things
9. cloud : white; colors
10. postal worker : mail; what people do
11. trees : woods; where they grow
12. brother : sister; male/female relatives
13. air : plane; where they move
14. desert : sand; what is found there
15. dog : bark; how they communicate
16. front : back; opposites

pages 8–9
Answers may vary in some cases.
1. sleep; where we do things
2. foot; where parts are found
3. play; where we do things
4. vet; what people do
5. hear; what they do
6. hop (or any rhyming word); rhymes
7. find or win; opposites
8. legs; where they are worn
9. read; what we do with things

pages 8–9 continued
10. road; where they move
11. burn; what they do
12. light; opposites
13. stamps; where we get things
14. book; what each sells
15. plate; how they are served
16. candy (or other sugary thing); how they taste
17. tide (or any other rhyming word); rhymes
18. rainy; opposites
19. rough; how they feel
20. hair; what we use to clean them
21. loud or noisy; opposites
22. chair or couch; where we find things
23. skate; where they are used
24. pull; synonyms

pages 10–11
Each answer completes the analogy.
1. second picture; small triangle
2. first picture; large six-sided figure
3. second picture; small smiley face
4. second picture; small cross
5. first picture; small oval
6. first picture; large tall rectangle
7. first picture; large right-facing triangle

pages 12–13
Check for correct colors. Each answer completes the analogy.
1. green triangle   4. yellow star
2. blue circle   5. blue moon
3. red diamond   6. black arrow

pages 14–15
Each answer completes the analogy.
1. second shape; triangle with design
2. second shape; plain circle
3. first shape; sideways design
4. second shape; designs in diamonds match designs in trapezoids
5. second shape; first pair shows a square straight, then with an X; rectangle straight, then with an X
6. second shape; first pair each contain a circle, second pair are same shapes with no circle

pages 16–17

1. A; pointing right and up
2. B; compares 2-D to 3-D figure
3. A; same shape with and without a border
4. A; a shape right-side-up and sideways
5. B; the same shape inverted and smaller
6. A; same shapes going in the same direction, but smaller

page 18

Check that correct choices were made and colored.

1. first shape; larger smaller relationship of same shape
2. first shape; larger/smaller relationship of same shape
3. first shape; same shape, different position
4. second shape; same shape shortened

pages 19–20

1. whole pizza; parts of a whole
2. park; where things are used
3. basketball hoop; where the balls are thrown
4. mail box; what we use things for
5. easel; what we use things for
6. fireplace; what things are made of

pages 21–22

1. D; where they live
2. C; what they produce
3. E; opposite sizes from like animal groups
4. C; how we use our senses
5. B; where they are worn
6. D; male/female adults and children

pages 23–24

1. clock; rhymes
2. horn; rhymes
3. snake; rhymes
4. bee; rhymes
5. whale; rhymes
6. nose; rhymes
7. squirrel; rhymes
8. cub; rhymes

pages 25–26

1. awake; opposites
2. sad; opposites
3. pull; opposites
4. wet; opposites
5. hard; opposites
6. sunny; opposites
7. noisy; opposites
8. hot; opposites

page 27

1. boy; female/male people
2. puppy; who these are treats for
3. tub; what happens there
4. skunk; what covers them

Stories will vary.

pages 28–29

1. look/feel; rough
2. what they do; cut
3. what they do; crawl
4. what they do; see
5. look/feel; cold
6. look/feel; yellow
7. what they do; taste

Analogy-Wiz

broom : sweep :: sponge : wash; what they do
night : dark :: day : light; how they look

pages 30–31

1. antonyms; slow
2. synonyms; go
3. synonyms; hear
4. antonyms; back
5. antonyms; ocean

Analogy-Wiz

blossom : flower :: dirt : soil; synonyms
left : right :: right : wrong; antonyms

pages 32–33

1. what it does; measure
2. what it's like; round
3. what it's like; mouse or frog
4. what it does; frog
5. what someone does; paint

Analogy-Wiz

hiker : walk :: diver : swim; what they do
summer : hot :: winter : cold; what they're like

page 34

1. flower : garden; growing things
2. deer : herd; parts of a group
3. page : book; parts of a whole related to reading/writing
4. dune : desert; landforms

page 35

1. d; male and female relatives
2. f; what they make
3. g; what they do
4. a; parts of a group
5. c; what they do
6. e; where they are found
7. h; how we use our senses
8. b; where things are done

page 36

1. e; what they produce
2. g; parts of a group
3. a or h; where they work
4. h or a; where they work
5. d; what they're like
6. c; what they do
7. b; opposites
8. f; synonyms

page 37

Across	Down
1. grasshopper	2. ant
6. butterfly	3. moth
	4. spider
	5. ladybug
	6. bee

page 38

Answers may vary. 1-4 tell where things are found.

1. bedroom
2. closet or bureau
3. lawn or yard
4. shed or garage
5. television; what we see or hear from things
6. talk; what we do with things

page 39

Answers may vary.
All refer to places on Earth.

1. desert
2. plains
3. ocean; sea; beach
4. sea; ocean
5. woods; forest
6. desert
7. desert
8. hot

page 40

Answers may vary.
1–5 are tools of a trade.

1. banker
2. baker
3. carpenter
4. paint (or other mediums)
5. ax
6. teacher; what they are in charge of

page 41

Answers may vary. All tell what things do.

1. cut
2. write
3. sweep
4. heat; bake; cook
5. turn
6. blow
7. dig
8. cut

page 42

Answers may vary. All tell what people do with or to things.

1. ride
2. drink
3. ride
4. rake
5. listen
6. pull

page 43

Answers may vary. All tell what people do with or to things.

1. swim
2. skate
3. brush
4. read
5. pitcher
6. play
7. pull
8. turn

page 44

Answers may vary. All describe things.

1. hot; how they feel
2. high; where they are
3. feathers; protective coverings
4. wrist; where things are found
5. fruit; what they are
6. square; their shape

page 45

Answers may vary. All describe things. 5–8 tell where things of similar purpose are found.

1. yellow; color
2. bark; coverings
3. swim; how they move
4. time; what they tell us
5. steering wheel
6. staple or paper clip
7. frame
8. ring